4/11   9⁰⁰

Monasticism in Egypt

Monasticism in Egypt

Images and Words of the Desert Fathers

Michael W. McClellan

With a Foreword
by
H.H. Pope Shenouda III

and
an Afterword
by
Otto F.A. Meinardus

The American University in Cairo Press

ontents

Acknowledgments

Completing the photographic work involved in this book would never have been possible without the help of some very dear Coptic friends. Traveling with me to remote desert locations during the hottest times of the Egyptian summer, staying in hotels and eating in restaurants that hardly merited their names, and hiking on foot through the desert sands on occasion to visit hidden caves and overlooks, these friends never flagged in their efforts and enthusiasm to help me realize this project and to convey to the outside world the essence and meaning of Coptic monasticism.

To Louis Fanous, many thanks for your organizational skills, contacts, and good cheer. To Magda Barsoum and Adel Beshai, thank you for your high spirits, your deep faith, and your personal interest in seeing this work through to its end. Adel, in particular, has proven to be a most excellent traveling companion in visits to other countries to visit Orthodox monasteries; thank you especially for your companionship and the many fruitful conversations we have shared over the years. To Maggie Kamel and Suzie Metry, thank you for helping to make arrangements wherever we went, for introducing me to innumerable monks and priests, and for always being in good humor no matter what the conditions of travel.

To all of you, my deepest appreciation for enabling me to experience one of Egypt's greatest gifts to the world and for helping me to penetrate a subject that is impenetrable to many.

This book is lovingly dedicated to my wife,
Tatiana Eugenevna McClellan,
and to my parents,
J. C. and May Evelyn McClellan

Foreword

"Love the Lord thy God with all thy heart, with all thy soul, and with all thy mind" (Matt. 22:37).

How can people love God with all their mind? With all their heart? Certainly we can love God through loving human beings. But the hermits of the early church wanted to forget the world, and to have only God and His love in their hearts and minds. They lived lifetimes without seeing another human being. There is a story in the *Paradise of the Fathers* about a monk walking in the desert, and on either side of him an angel. But the monk did not look to his left or his right. "I do not want even angels to interrupt my meditation on God," he said.

For these hermits and monks, God was the unique focus of their lives. They were known as "angels on earth." In St. Luke's gospel (18:1) it is written "And He spake a parable unto them to this end, that men ought always to pray, and not to faint." In the First Epistle to the Thessalonians 5:17, we are told to "pray without ceasing." These are the commands they set out to obey.

After the first centuries of monasticism, many monks were called out of the desert to work for the church as priests and pastors. But some remained in solitude. When our Lord God was about to burn the city of Sodom, He said that if he were to find just ten pure persons living there, then He would relent and spare the city. Today, as then, we need people to carry on that life of purity.

In the past there were hundreds of monasteries in Egypt. Now there are far fewer, but monastic life is returning to the desert. We have built cells for the new monks, and retreat houses for people who would like to spend short periods at the monasteries. In Sunday schools we prepare our children to live spiritual lives. Some of them will go on to become monks, others will become priests, others will serve God in the world in other ways. But the monastic option, and the monastic calling is always there. If you visit our monasteries, you will be warmly welcomed, and you will see how an ancient tradition is still alive today.

H.H. Pope Shenouda III
Patriarch of Alexandria and the See of Saint Mark

Introduction

Christian monasticism began in Egypt, and it is to Egypt's parched deserts that all Orthodox, Roman Catholic, and Protestant monastic movements trace their lineage. This book is about the Egyptian desert and the Coptic Orthodox Church, which has preserved the indigenous monastic tradition for over sixteen hundred years.

Dividing the Egyptian desert is the Nile, a river whose banks nurtured one of the world's greatest civilizations. Beyond those banks lie the barren wastes where the simple, often illiterate, followers of an unseen God gave birth to another civilization, one not of this world—the unworldly world of monasticism.

I first became interested in monasticism as a teenager growing up in central Kentucky near the Roman Catholic Monastery of Gethsemane. Although I was born into a Southern Baptist family, I felt very attracted to Gethsemane and went there often on Sundays to listen to the services and the soft Gregorian chants for which the monks are famous.

I was also drawn to the simplicity of the church itself, its sparse decorations, the simple stall where each monk stood quietly in his plain, white robe and black belt. I never got to know any of those fathers, but I wanted desperately to learn more about their way of life.

In the late 1970s, as a student of photojournalism, I encountered Russian Orthodox monasticism. As part of a photographic documentary project, I visited the Holy Trinity Russian Orthodox Monastery in Jordanville, New York, where a large group of predominantly Russian immigrant monks were living the monastic life according to the Russian tradition. There was much in common between the life they lived and the life of the Trappist fathers at Gethsemane.

On the refectory wall, painted in the Russian style with Old Slavonic inscriptions, were beautiful frescoes, many of them depicting sandy deserts and empty wastes—scenes I knew were not Russian. The fathers explained to me the pictures of St. Mary of Egypt, St. Anthony the Great, St. Paul of Thebes, and others. Strange, I thought, that Russian monks would feel so close to Egypt, a land so different from their own. As I delved deeper into the subject, however, I began to understand why; the movement had begun not in Europe or Russia, but in Egypt. My interest in monasticism, which had first grown in the green hills of Kentucky, was to come into full flower in the empty expanses of the Egyptian desert.

My first visit to an Egyptian monastery was on a day tour to Wadi al-Natrun, where today four active monasteries remain out of the hundreds that existed in the fourth and fifth centuries. These holy places, striking as they were, did not touch me then as they would on subsequent visits. The crowded tour bus, the lightning-fast guided tours, and the noise and push of countless visitors and pilgrims precluded the kind of spiritual experience I had hoped for. My second trip was to the monasteries of St. Paul of Thebes and St. Anthony the Great in the Red Sea Desert. This trip, private and unhurried, at a time when few other visitors were present, was my first real encounter with the monks and monasteries of Egypt.

A few kilometers from the Red Sea coast of Egypt, surrounded by desert and mountains, is the Monastery of St. Paul of Thebes. Small, rustic, built of mud-brick, and baked for centuries by the desert sun, this monastery is perhaps the ultimate symbol of the simple, austere monasticism of the Egyptian desert. Home of Christianity's first hermit, this beautiful, holy place has quietly stood firm and unchanging in a world of constant upheaval.

About thirty kilometers from St. Paul's is another of Egypt's holiest places, the Monastery of St. Anthony the Great. A little older than the Monastery of St. Paul of Thebes, it is considerably larger and more prosperous, yet the sense of holiness that pervades it is just as strong and just as sweet as that of St. Paul's. St. Anthony's monastery is built at the foot of a mountain, near the cave where St. Anthony spent forty years in solitude and prayer, developing the way of life that would lead him and countless followers in subsequent centuries to communion with God. The cave is high up on a cliff face above the monastery. This narrow fissure in the stone face of the mountain is a monument to the inner struggle and ascetic lives of St. Anthony and the generations of men and women since who have been inspired by his example.

At the top of the stairway that leads to the cave is a small rock platform, a natural resting place scarcely more than twenty or thirty square meters in area. Here, the weary pilgrim can rest and contemplate a panorama that has changed little in sixteen centuries. Most of what one sees today is what St. Anthony saw when he sat weaving baskets or mats, or watching the sun rise after a night spent in prayer.

On the cliff face above the platform are dozens of crosses, some painted on the rock, some made of sticks placed in cracks, and some made of stones arranged on the sloping rock. There are also Arabic inscriptions, some quoting St. Anthony, others asking for his prayers, others recording a pilgrim's visit.

At the back of the platform is an opening in the cliff face, barely more than a crack. Because this is a holy place, pilgrims remove their shoes before proceeding into the dark cave. By turning sideways, one can squeeze into the tiny passage. After three or four meters there is a sharp turn to the right. Another meter or two and the passage opens into a tiny room, barely three square meters in size.

Were it not for a few candles burning, the room would be almost totally dark. A few rays of sunlight crawl through the passage , but they do little to illuminate the dark walls of the cave. By the light of a single candle, however, every crack and contour of the room can be seen. To me, it looked familiar; I had seen it before on the refectory wall of the Russian Orthodox monks in New York.

According to the *Lives* of Saints Anthony and Paul of Thebes, the two Holy Fathers met for the first time shortly before St. Paul died. St. Anthony recorded the life of St. Paul, who had also struggled in solitude for the previous forty years, unknown to St. Anthony, just thirty kilometers away .

The cave of St. Paul is now the altar of an ancient, underground church in the center of the Monastery of St. Paul of Thebes. When I first visited the monastery, I fell in love with it, and I have returned there many times—and hope to do so again and again. Although I have visited dozens of monasteries throughout the Orthodox world, most of them far richer, more elaborate, and more elegant, for me St. Paul's will always be an especially holy place, with far more spiritual significance than mere appearances might indicate. More, perhaps, than any other monastery in the world, this simple, austere monastery, with its discipline and ascetic rule, symbolizes the special monasticism of the Eastern churches. In the course of many visits to nearly all of Egypt's monasteries, St. Paul's always calls me back, and every time it speaks to me in a new and different way of the need for monasticism in the modern world.

The church of St. Paul, built around his cave, fills me with awe and inspires in me a feeling of repentance and wonder that can be found only in such holy places. Much enlarged from the original hole in the desert floor, the altar is still too small for a person of average height to stand erect in.The altar and the church itself are painted with centuries-old frescoes done in that primitive, child-like style for which the Copts are so famous, and which reflects the simplicity and innocence of the Coptic faith, a faith that stands unchanged from the earliest times of Christianity.

St. Paul is considered Christianity's first hermit, but to St. Anthony is credited the founding of a type of monasticism that might be called 'communal heremeticism.' This way of life was typical of the monks of Wadi al-Natrun and the Red Sea Desert. In these small communities, numbers of monks ranging from a handful to several dozen lived in isolated dwellings throughout the week, coming together only on Saturdays and Sundays for church services, Holy Communion, a communal meal, and teachings from fathers considered wiser and more experienced. In these communal gatherings a 'word' would be spoken—sometimes a sermon, sometimes a few sentences, sometimes literally just a word. Such grains of thought coming from holy men were enough to keep the monks nourished for the coming week and by meditating upon them in silence they would grow in wisdom and spirit. At the end of their time together, they would return to their caves alone, often taking provisions sufficient for the coming week and leaving behind them the baskets, mats, or other handicrafts they had made. Even today, as one drives up the Nile Valley toward Asyut and beyond, the remains of thousands of hermit caves can be seen in the mountains, square holes cut into the rock just big enough to accommodate one man and a few provisions.

In Upper Egypt, however, a different form of monastic life developed that was to have a more profound effect on the development of monasticism. This was the 'cenobitic' life espoused by St. Pachomius the Great. In this type of community, the monks live together and share all property in common. Church services are held daily, duties (or obediences) are assigned to each father, and daily life is carefully structured. As monasticism spread from Egypt to Palestine and Syria and from there to the Byzantine Empire, the Roman West, Eastern Europe, and eventually to Russia, both the cenobitic and eremetic ways were followed, but it was always the cenobitic life that predominated.

At the Red and White Monasteries of Sohag, one can see many pieces of ancient, pagan temples used in the construction of Christian structures. Even before the Christian period the area was profoundly religious, with hundreds of temples to many different gods and goddesses scattered across the desert landscape and throughout the Nile Valley. With the advent of Christianity, thousands of Egyptians took up the monastic life, rejecting the world and its pagan values, until the Egyptian desert became so filled with monks that John Cassian reported in the fifth century that one could travel through the Western Desert from Alexandria to Thebes and hear the singing of hymns the entire way.

From all over Europe, men and women seeking holiness flocked to Egypt as birds migrating south. Virtually every monastic founder from the early centuries visited Egypt and lived in its deserts at least for a while, learning of the monastic way and imbibing its discipline, before returning home and spreading the monastic message along the way. Egypt's influence can also be seen in Russia, a country that converted to Christianity centuries after the glorious early years of Egyptian monasticism. The founding father of Russia's first monastery, the Kiev Caves Lavra (a lavra is a large monastery), was St.

Anthony of Kiev, who lived as a hermit first in a cave on Greece's Mount Athos and then in a cave near Kiev overlooking the Dnieper River. As monasticism flowered in Russia (by 1917 there were over a thousand monasteries and more than one hundred thousand monks), it came to be known as the 'Northern Thebes.'

This book deals with the monasticism of the Coptic Church, and also with the Greek Orthodox Monastery of St. Catherine at Mount Sinai. Dr. Otto Meinardus, a world-renowned authority on the Coptic Church, has contributed a chapter outlining the history and development of Coptic monasticism. For a more in-depth study, Dr. Meinardus's book *Monks and Monasteries of the Egyptian Deserts* is unsurpassed.

Most of the book, however, is devoted to photographs of the monks and the lives they lead. Some of the images are also from the Greek Orthodox Monastery of St. Catherine in Sinai which, though not Coptic, is nevertheless a vital part of Egypt's monastic history and a site of pilgrimage for many Coptic and foreign pilgrims. The photographs are accompanied by words from the ancient desert fathers and together they demonstrate the continuity of spirit and thought that characterizes this movement and the lives of the men and women who live by it today . The book is intended to provide the reader with an introduction to the inner monastic life as it is practiced in Egypt and to add a visual perspective to the wisdom of the ancient desert fathers. It is the hope of the author that through this book the reader will gain an appreciation of the wisdom of the ancient desert fathers, and understand something of their history and the movement they inspired and which lives on today..

For over sixteen centuries, the still, small voice of Egypt's monks has spoken to the world. It can still be heard today, even amid the noise and bustle of the twentieth century. It will speak to each of us, it will touch each of us, it will guide each of us—but only if we stop and listen. Take time to stop. Listen carefully. The voice is speaking.

Images and Words

of the

Desert Fathers

A certain man said that there were once three men who loved labours, and they were monks. The first one chose to go about and see where there was strife, which he turned into peace; the second chose to go about and visit the sick; but the third departed to the desert that he might dwell in quietness. Finally the first man, who had chosen to still the contentions of men, was unable to make every man to be at peace with his neighbor, and his spirit was sad; and he went to the man who had chosen to visit the sick, and he found him in affliction because he was not able to fulfil the law which he had laid down for himself. Then the two of them went to the monk in the desert, and seeing each other they rejoiced, and the two men related to the third the tribulations which had befallen them in the world, and entreated him to tell them how he had lived in the desert. And he was silent, but after a little he said unto them, "Come, let each of us go and fill a vessel of water"; and after they had filled the vessel, he said unto them, "Pour out some of the water into a basin, and look down to the bottom through it," and they did so. And he said unto them, "What do ye see?" and they said, "We see nothing." And after the water in the basin had ceased to move, he said to them a second time, "Look into the water," and they looked, and he said unto them, "What do ye see?" And they said unto him, "We see our own faces distinctly"; and he said unto them, "Thus is it with the man who dwelleth with men, for by reason of the disturbance caused by this affair of the world he cannot see his sins; but if he live in the peace and quietness of the desert he is able to see God clearly."

Bell-tower and Church of St. Michael the Archangel, Monastery of St. Paul of Thebes.

Brother: What kind of labour should the heart perform?

Old Man: The perfect labour of monks is for a man
to have his gaze directed towards God
firmly and continually.

Monk with icon, Monastery of St. Paul of Thebes.

Abbâ John used to say, "The whole company of the holy men is like unto a garden which is full of fruit-bearing trees of various kinds, and wherein the trees are planted in [one] earth, and all of them drink from one fountain; and thus is it with all the holy men, for they have not one rule only, but several varieties, and one man laboureth in one way, and another man in another, but it is one Spirit which operateth and worketh in them."

Overview of the garden of the Monastery of St. Paul of Thebes.

On one occasion certain brethren went to Abbâ Agathon, because they had heard that he took the greatest possible care that his mind should not be disturbed by anything, and they sought to try him, and to see if his mind would rise [to any matter]; and they said unto him, "Art thou indeed Agathon? We have heard that thou art a whoremonger and a boastful man." And Agathon said unto them, "Yea, I am." And again they said unto him, "Agathon, thou art a garrulous and talkative old man"; and he said unto them, "Indeed I am." And again they said unto him, "Agathon, thou art a heretic"; and he said unto them, "I am not a heretic." Then they said unto him, "Tell us now why in answer to all these things which we have said to thee thou hast replied, 'Yea,' and that thou hast endured them all with the exception of the accusation of being a heretic." Abbâ Agathon said unto them, "The earlier things I accounted as profitable to my soul, but heresy meaneth separation from God, and I do not wish to be separated from God." And when the brethren heard [these words] they marvelled at his solicitude, and went away rejoicing.

A cross and an icon,
Monastery of St. Paul
of Thebes.

A brother asked an old man, and said unto him, "Supposing that I find sufficient for
my daily wants in any place, dost thou wish me not to take care for the work of my hands?"
The old man said unto him, "However much thou mayest have, do
not neglect the work of thy hands; work as much as
thou canst, only do not work with
an agitated mind."

At work in the carpentry shop, Monastery of St. Paul of Thebes.

Abbâ Agathon said concerning Abbâ Muain that, on one occasion, he made fifty bushels of wheat into bread for the needs of the community, and then laid it out in the sun, but before it became dry and hard he saw something in the place which was not helpful to him, and he said to the brethren who were with him, "Arise, let us go hence"; and they were greatly grieved. And when he saw that they were grieved, he said unto them, "Are ye troubled about the bread? Verily I have seen men take to flight and forsake their cells, although they were well whitewashed and contained cupboards which were filled with books of the Holy Scriptures and service books, and they did not even shut the cupboard doors, but departed leaving them wide open."

Baking bread in the Monastery of St. Paul of Thebes.

A certain old man used to dwell with a brother in a cell in a friendly manner, and he was a man of compassionate disposition; now a famine broke out, and the people began to be hungry, and they came to him that they might receive charity, and he gave bread unto them all. And when the brother saw that he was giving away large quantities of bread, he said unto the old man, "Give me my portion of the bread," and the old man said unto him, "Take [it]," and he divided [what there was] and gave him [his share], and the brother took it from him for himself. And the old man was compassionate, and gave away bread from his portion, and many folk heard [that he was doing this] and came unto him, and when God saw the generosity of the old man He blessed his bread; but the brother took all his portion and ate it up, and when he saw that his bread was finished, and that the portion of the old man was still lasting, he made entreaty unto him, saying, "My portion hath come to an end, and this [bread of thine is all] that I have; receive me as a partner [therein]." And the old man said unto him, "Good," and he associated him with himself again. And when there was abundance [again], the people came to take [bread] from him, and he gave it unto them again. Now it came to pass that they lacked bread, and the brother went and found that bread was wanting, and a poor man came for some, and the old man said unto the brother, "Go in and give him some," and the brother said, "There is none"; for he was filled with bread. The old man said, "Go in and search [for some]," and having gone in he found that the place wherein they used to set [the bread] was filled with loaves to the very top, and he took [some] and gave to the poor man, and he was afraid. Thus that brother knew the excellence and the faith of the old man, and he gave thanks unto God, and glorified Him.

Preparing the dough for baking bread, Monastery of St. Paul of Thebes.

On one occasion Abbâ Moses of Pâtârâ was engaged in a war against fornication, and he could not endure being in his cell, and he went and informed Abbâ Isidore of it; and the old man entreated him to return to his cell, but he would not agree [to this]. And having said, "Father, I cannot bear it," the old man took him up to the roof of his cell, and said unto him, "Look to the west," and when he looked he saw multitudes of devils with troubled and terrified aspects, and they shewed themselves in the forms of phantoms which were in fighting attitudes. Abbâ Isidore saith unto him, "Look to the east," and when he looked he saw innumerable holy angels standing [there], and they were in a state of great glory. Then Abbâ Isidore said unto him, "Behold, those who are in the west are those who are fighting with the holy ones, and those whom thou hast seen in the east are they who are sent by God to the help of the saints, for those who are with us are many." And having seen [these] Abbâ Moses took courage and returned to his cell without fear.

Keep, Monastery of St. Paul of Thebes.

An old man said, "Whensoever a man readeth
the Divine Books, the devils
are afraid."

Reading an ancient manuscript, Monastery of St. Paul of Thebes.

They used to say that Abbâ Sylvanus had in Scete a disciple whose name was Mark, and that he possessed to a great degree the faculty of obedience; he was a scribe, and the old man loved him greatly for his obedience. Now Sylvanus had eleven other disciples, and they were vexed because they saw that the old man loved Mark more than them, and when the old men who were in Scete heard [of this] they were afflicted about it. And one day when they came to him to reprove him about this, Sylvanus took them, and went forth, and passing by the cells of the brethren, he knocked at the door of each cell, and said, "O brother, come forth, for I have need of thee"; and he quickly passed by all their cells, and not one of them obeyed him quickly. But when they went to the cell of Mark, he knocked at the door and said, "Brother Mark," and as soon as Mark heard the voice of the old man, he jumped up straightway, and came out, and Sylvanus sent him off on some business. Then Sylvanus said unto the old men, "My fathers, where are the other brethren?" And they went into Mark's cell, and looked at the quire of the book which he was writing, and they saw that he had begun to write [one side of] the Greek letter o (or w), and that as soon as he heard the voice of his master, [he ran out] and did not stay to complete the other side of the letter. Now when the old men perceived these things, they answered and said unto Sylvanus, "Verily, O old man, we also love the brother whom thou lovest, for God also loveth him."

Illuminated manuscript, Monastery of St. Paul of Thebes.

They used to say about Abbâ Arsenius that no man was able to attain to the manner of life in his abode. And they also said about him that on the night of the Sabbâth which would end in the dawn of Sunday, he would leave the sun behind him, and would stretch out his hands towards heaven, and would pray [in this position] until the sunrose in his face, when he would satisfy his eyes with a little slumber.

Shadow on dome, Monastery of St. Paul of Thebes.

One of the monks wished to go out from his monastery and to wander about so that he might
have a little relaxation and enjoyment, and when they saw him, an old man
said, himunto "Seek not gratification in this world, O my son,
but work rather and persevere therein in the
invincible power of the Holy Trinity."

30

Overview of the Monastery of St. Paul of Thebes.

Abbâ Anthony said, "As a fish when it is lifted up out of the water dieth, even so doth the monk who tarrieth outside his cell."

Keep and bell-towers, Monastery of St. Anthony the Great.

A disciple of Abbâ Ammon told the following story: "On one occasion when we were singing the service, my mind became confused, and I forgot the verse in the Psalm; and when we had ended the service Ammon answered and said unto me, 'Whilst I was standing up during the service it seemed that I was standing on fire and was being consumed, and my mind was unable to make me turn aside either to the right hand or to the left. And as for thee, where was thy mind when we were singing the service? for thou didst omit a verse from the Psalm. Didst thou not know that thou wast standing in the presence of God, and that thou wast speaking unto him?'"

*Church door at Easter,
Monastery of St. Anthony
the Great.*

Abbâ Arsenius used to repeat this saying, "That I have spoken I have many times repented; that I held my peace I have never repented."

Monk, Monastery
of St. Anthony the Great.

The fathers prophesied concerning the later generation, saying, "What manner of work will they do?" And one of them, whose conduct was exalted, and whose name was Isôkhôrôn, said, "We perform the commandments of God"; and the others answered and said unto him, "And those who will come after us, what manner of work will they do?" And he said, "They will attain to the half of our service." And again they answered and said, "What manner of work will those who come after these do?" And he said, "Those who are in that generation will possess no work of any kind, for many trials are about to come upon them, and those among them who are found to be chosen men will be found to be greater than ourselves and our fathers."

Two African Roman Catholic monks visit the cave of St. Anthony the Great.

A brother asked an old man and said, "What shall I do? For there is no feeling in my soul, and I have no fear of God." The old man said unto him, "Seek thou out a man who feareth God, and then cling closely to him, and from him thou shalt learn to fear God."

Cliff-face above the cave of St. Anthony.

A certain woman who was afflicted in her lungs with the disease called cancer, heard concerning Longinus and wished to see him; now he used to dwell in [the monastery of] Hantôn in Alexandria. And whilst the woman was seeking and wishing for him, it happened that the blessed man was gathering sticks on the sea-shore, and when the woman found him, she said unto him, "Father, where dwelleth the man of God, Abbâ Longinus?" Now she did not know that he himself was Longinus. And he said unto her, "What dost thou want with that lying hypocrite? Do not go to him, for he is a liar. What is it that causeth thee pain?" Then the woman shewed him the place, and the old man made the sign of the Cross over it, and he dismissed her, saying, "Go, and may our Lord heal thee, for Longinus is unable to do thee any good whatsoever." And the woman went away believing in the word, and she was healed straightway; and afterwards, when she was telling folks the story, she

said, "I have learned by the marks which were on

the old man that he himself was

Abbâ Longinus."

Wave and rock, Alexandria.

A certain monk . . . was gracious unto every man in his humility, and all the brethren marvelled at his abstinence from meats; then he went to the barren desert, and lived there for many years, eating for food wild herbs. And afterwards he entreated God to inform him what reward He would give him, and it was said unto him by an angel, "Go forth from this desert and get thee along the road, and behold a certain shepherd shall meet thee, and according to [what he saith] so shalt thou receive." Now when he had made ready to depart, the shepherd . . . met him, and saluted him, and having sat down to hold converse with each other, the monk saw in the shepherd's bag some green herbs, and he asked him saying, "What is this?" And the shepherd said unto him, "It is my food." And the monk said unto him, "How long hast thou been feeding thyself on these green herbs?" And the shepherd said unto him, "Behold, for the last thirty years, more or less, and I have never tasted anything else except these herbs which I have eaten once a day, and I drink as much water as my food requireth; and the wages which are given to me by the owner of the sheep I give unto the poor." Now when the monk heard these things he said, "I imagined that I had laid hold upon abstinence, but thou through thy well-ordered life art worthy of a greater reward than I, because I have eaten every kind of green thing immediately it came in my way." Then the shepherd said unto him, "It is not right that rational men should make themselves like unto the beasts, but they should eat whatsoever is prepared for them at the seasons which are duly ordered and appointed for them, and afterwards they should fast from everything until an appointed time."

And the monk profited by these words, . . . and marvelled how many were the saints in the world who were not known to the children of men.

Cave of Pope Cyril VI, Monastery of al-Baramus.

A certain stranger came to Scete, and brought there much gold, and he entreated the priest that it might be given to the brethren, and the priest said unto him, "It is useless to them"; and having entreated him many times, and the priest not consenting to this, the man laid the gold down openly at the door of the church. And the priest said, "My brethren, if any man hath need let him take [some]," but they refused to touch it, and some of them would not even look at it. Then the priest said unto him, "God hath accepted thy gift, go, and give it to the poor"; and having been greatly helped he departed.

View from the keep, Monastery of al-Baramus.

A brother asked an old man and said, "Why is it that when I go forth to labour I feel wearied and disgusted in my soul, and my mind is wholly empty of spiritual thoughts?" And the old man said unto him, "Because thou dost not desire to fulfil that which is written, I will bless the Lord always, and His praises shall be ever in my mouth' (Psalm XXXIV, I). Therefore, whether thou art inside or outside, and whithersoever thou goest thou must not cease from blessing God; not only in actions, but with word and mind thou shalt bless thy Maker. For God doth not dwell in any place which hath bounds and limits, but He is everywhere, and by His Divine Power He sustaineth all things, and is capable of all things."

Monk on bench, Monastery of al-Baramus.

They used to say that Abbâ Macarius the Alexandrian at one time dwelt in a cave in the desert, and that beyond his cave was another wherein dwelt a panther; one day when he opened the door of his cave the panther came in and did homage to the blessed man, and she drew nigh and took hold of the corner of his garment, and dragged him along gently and went outside. And the old man answered and said, "What can this animal want?" And he went with her until she arrived at her cave, and she left him outside, and went in and brought out her young, which were blind and dropped them at his feet; and when he saw them, he prayed, and spat in their eyes, which were opened straightway, and the panther gave them suck, and took them and went inside. And on the day following the panther came bringing a sheepskin, and she approached and placed it before him; then the old man smiled to himself at the discernment and knowledge which the animal had shewn, and he took the skin and slept upon it, until it was quite worn out.

A hermitage near the Monastery of St. Macarius.

A brother asked Abbâ Ammon, saying, "Behold, there were two men, the one was a monk, and the other a son of the world; now the monk used to determine in the evening to cast away from him in the morning the garb of the monk, and the son of the world used to make up his mind that on the morrow he would take the garb of monkhood. Now it happened that both men died on the same night; how will they be regarded, and which determination will be reckoned to them?" The old man said unto him, "He who was a monk died a monk, and he who was a child of the world died as such, for as they were found [to be] so were they taken."

Steps and shadows, Monastery of St. Macarius.

A certain brother came to Abbâ Macarius, the Egyptian, and said unto him, "Father, speak to me a word whereby I may live." Abbâ Macarius saith unto him, "Get thee to the cemetery and revile the dead"; and he went and reviled them, and stoned them with stones, and he came and informed the old man [that he had done so]. And the old man said unto him, "Did they say nothing unto thee?" and the brother said unto him, "No." And again the old man said unto him, "Go to-morrow and praise them, and call them, 'Apostles, Saints, and Righteous Men'"; and he came to the old man, and said, "I have praised them." And the old man said unto him, "And did they return thee no answer?" and he said, "No." And the old man said unto him, "Thou seest how thou hast praised them, and that they said nothing to thee, and that although thou didst revile them they returned thee no answer. And thus let it be with thyself.
If thou wishest to live, become dead, so that thou mayest care neither
for the reviling of men nor for [their] praise, for the dead
care for nothing; in this wise thou
wilt be able to live."

Monastery of St. Samuel.

And I asked him also, "In what doth the power of exile consist?" And he said unto me,
"Wheresoever thou dwellest hold thy peace; and about whatsoever thou seest, be it good or be
it evil, say nothing; and if thou hearest anything from a man which befitteth
not the upright conduct of the ascetic life, say, 'This concerneth
me not; I have to do with myself, and myself only.'
This is [the power of] exile."

Interior of the Church of the Holy Family, Durunka.

On one occasion the Arabs came and plundered Abbâ Sisoes and the brother who was with him of everything they had, and being hungry, the brethren went out into the desert to find something to eat. And when they were some distance from each other, Abbâ Sisoes found some camel dung, and he broke it, and found inside two grains of barley; and he ate one grain and placed the other in his hand; and when the brother came, and found that he was eating, he said unto him, "Is this love? Thou hast found food, and thou eatest it by thyself and hast not called me [to share it with thee]." Abbâ Sisoes saith unto him, "I have not defrauded thee, O brother, for behold, I have kept thy share in my hands."

*Bishop Andrawus, Church
of the Holy Family, Durunka.*

An old man was asked by one who toiled, "Is the repentance of sinners accepted by God?" And the old man, after he had taught him with many words, said unto him, "Tell me, O my beloved one: if thy cloak were to be torn in rags, wouldst thou throw it away?" And he said unto him, "No, but I would sew up the rents, and then I could use it again." And the old man said unto him, "If thou wouldst shew pity upon thy garment which hath no feeling, shall not God shew pity on that which He hath fashioned, and which is His work?"

Church interior,
White Monastery, Sohag.

They say that Abbâ Hôr of the Cells dwelt for twenty years in
the church, and that he never once lifted his eyes
and saw the roof thereof.

Church dome, Red Monastery, Sohag.

When Abbâ Sisoes was about to die, and the fathers were sitting about him, they saw that his face was shining like the sun; and he said unto them straightway, "Behold, Abbâ Anthony hath come"; and after a little while he said also, "Behold, the company of the prophets hath come"; his face shone again, and he said, "Behold the company of apostles hath come"; and again his face shone with twofold brightness, and he became suddenly like unto one who was speaking with some one. Then the old men who were sitting [there] entreated him, and said, "Show us with whom thou art talking, father"; and straightway he said unto them, "Behold, the angels came to take me away, and I besought them to leave me so that I might tarry here a little longer, and repent." And the old men said unto him, "Thou hast no need to repent, father"; the old man said unto them, "I do not know in my soul if I have rightly begun to repent"; and they all learned that the old man was perfect. Then again suddenly his face beamed like the sun, and all who sat there were afraid, and he said unto them straightway, "Look ye, look ye. Behold our Lord hath come, and He saith, 'Bring ye unto Me the chosen vessel which is in the desert"; and straightway he delivered up his spirit, and he became [like] lightning, and the whole place was filled with a sweet odour.

Monk in church, Red Monastery, Sohag.

An old man from Thebaïs used to say: I was the son of a priest of idols, and when I was young I lived in the temple, and I have on many occasions seen my father go into the temple to perform the sacrifices to the idols. Once I went in secretly after him, and I saw Satan sitting [there], with his whole army before him, and, behold, one of his devils came and did homage to him. And Satan answered and said unto him, "Whence comest thou?" And the devil made answer, saying, "I was in such and such a country, and I stirred up many wars and revolts, and I caused the shedding of blood, and I have come to tell thee these things." Satan said unto him, "How long did it take thee to do this?" and the devil said "Thirty days." Then Satan commanded him to be beaten, saying unto him, "Is this all that thou hast done in so long a time?" . . . Then afterwards, behold, [another] devil came and worshipped him, and Satan answered and said unto him, "And whence comest thou also?" And he who was asked answered and said unto him, "I have been in the desert for forty years striving with a monk, and to-night I have hurled him into fornication"; And when Satan heard this, he rose up straightway and embraced and kissed that devil, and he took the crown off his head, and placed it upon him, and he made him to sit by his side upon his throne, saying, "And so thou hast been able to do so great a work as this in so short a time! For there is nothing which I prize so highly as the fall of a monk." And the old man went on to say: When I saw these things I said within myself, "Yea, so great then is the army of the monks!

And by the operation of God, Who desired my

redemption, I came forth, and

became a monk."

Temple of Karnak, Luxor.

There were two men in the desert who were brethren in the flesh, and a devil came to separate them from each other; and one day the younger brother lit a lamp and set it upon a candlestick, but, by the agency of the Evil One, he overturned the candlestick and extinguished the lamp. Then the elder brother was angry and smote him, and the younger brother made excuses to him, saying, "Have a little patience with me, and I will light the lamp again." Now when God saw his patient endurance, He punished that devil until the morning, and the devil came and told the prince of devils what had happened; and there was with the prince of devils a certain priest of idols, and straightway this man left everything, and he went and became a monk. And at the very beginning he laid hold upon humility, saying, "Humility is able to bring to naught all the power of the Adversary, even as I have heard from the devils, who said, 'Whensoever we stir up the monks, they turn to humility, and they make excuses one to the other, and thus they do away all our power.'"

Temple of Karnak, Luxor.

And he also said, "As fish die when they are drawn out of the water, even so do monks, who have forsaken the world, become sluggish, when they remain with the children of this world or dwell with them; it is then meet for us to haste to the mountain even as fish hasten to the water."

The Greek Orthodox Monastery of St. Catherine at the foot of Mount Sinai.

On one occasion a certain brother came to Mount Sinai to visit Abbâ Sylvanus, and he saw the brethren working with their hands to supply their wants, and he said unto Abbâ Sylvanus, with boasting, "Ye toil for the food which perisheth; Mary chose a good portion for herself." Then Abbâ Sylvanus said unto Zechariah, his disciple, "Give him a book and take him to a cell wherein there is nothing." And when the time of the ninth hour had come, the brother looked this way and that way to see if they were going to send for him to come and eat, but no man came to seek him. Then he rose up and came to the old man and said unto him, "Father, have not the brethren eaten to-day?" And he said unto him, "Yea." And the brother said unto him, "Why have ye not called me?" The old man said unto him, "Thou art a spiritual man and hast no need of the meat which is for the body, but we are corporeal beings, and we require to eat, and it is for this reason that we work. Thou hast chosen the [good] part; read all day, and do not seek after the food of the body." Now when that brother heard [this] he expressed his contrition, and said, "Father, forgive me"; and
the old man said, "Even Mary had need of Martha,
for through the labour of Martha
Mary triumphed."

Church interior, Monastery of St. Catherine, Sinai.

And when a philosopher asked him how he could endure without books his long solitude,
[St. Anthony] would point to the mountainous wilderness around him:
"My book, O philosopher, is the nature of created things,
and it is present when I will, for me to
read the words of God."

74

The peak of Mount Sinai.

One of the fathers said, "God beareth with the sins of those who
live in the world, but He will not endure the sins
of those who live in the desert."

Church of St. George, on the trail between the Monastery of St. Catherine and Mount Sinai.

A certain old man dwelt in the desert at a distance of ten miles from the monastery, where-from he had always to draw water, and on one occasion the matter became very wearisome to him, and he said, "What is the necessity for me to labour so much? I will come and will take up my abode by the side of this stream." And having said this, he turned behind him and he saw a man coming after him, and he was counting his footsteps, and he asked him, saying, "Who art thou?" And he answered and said unto him, "I am an angel of the Lord, and I have been sent to count thy footsteps, and to give thee thy reward"; and having heard this the old man was consoled greatly, and he went five miles further from the place wherein he was, and took up his abode there.

A small stream in the desert near the Monastery of St. Catherine, Sinai.

An old man said, "The Calumniator is the Enemy, and the Enemy will never cease to cast
into thy house, if he possibly can, impurity of every kind, and it is thy duty neither to refuse
nor to neglect to take that which is cast in and to throw it out; for if thou art negligent thy house
will become filled with impurity, and thou wilt be unable to enter therein. Therefore
whatsoever the Enemy casteth in little by little do thou throw out
little by little, and thy house shall remain pure
by the Grace of Christ."

Hermitage in the desert near the Monastery of St. Catherine, Sinai.

On one occasion thieves came to the cell of an old man, and said unto him, "We have come to take away everything which thou hast in thy cell"; and he said unto them, "My sons, take whatsoever ye please"; and they took everything which they saw in his cell and departed. Now they forgot [to take] a wallet which was hanging there, and the old man took it and ran after them, and entreated them, saying, "My sons, take this wallet which ye have left behind in your cell." And when the thieves saw this they marvelled at the good disposition of the old man, and they gave back everything which they had taken from his cell, and they repented, and said to each other, "Verily, this man is a man of God."

Hermitage in the desert near the Monastery of St. Catherine, Sinai.

They used to say that when Abbâ Macarius was walking in the desert, he went and found a beautiful spot which was like unto the Paradise of God; and there were in it fountains of water, and numerous palm trees, and trees of various kinds which bore fruit, and when he had come and told the brethren about it, they begged and entreated him to go and settle them there. Then the old men, the aged members of the congregation, who led lives of stern labour, entreated them not to leave their place, and they said, "If pleasure and delight be found in that spot, and if a man may live therein without vexation and labour, what pleasure and delight do ye expect to receive from God? Nay, it is right for us to endure the hardness of this place wherein we dwell, and to suffer tribulations so that we may enjoy pleasure in the world to come." And when he had said these things thebrethren were restrained and departed not.

*Icon corner of a hermitage
in the desert near the Monastery
of St. Catherine, Sinai.*

A certain brother asked an old man a question, and said unto him, "Father, what shall I do? For, although my body is in my cell, my thoughts wander about into every place, and because of this they vex me greatly, saying, 'Thou hast no benefit whatsoever, for though thy body is shut up in the cell, thy thoughts wander and are scattered abroad.' And they bring me to despair, and counsel me to go back to the world as one who has not the ability to acquire the rule of life which is proper for the ascetic monk." The old man said unto him, "Thou must know, O my son, that this is an attack of Satan, but go, and continue to abide in thy cell, and go not out of it at any time, and pray to God that He may give thee the power to endure patiently, and then thy mind shall collect itself in thee. For the matter is like unto that of a she-ass which hath a sucking foal. If she be tied up, however much the foal may gambol about or wander hither and thither, he will come back to her eventually, either because he is hungry, or for other reasons which drive him to her; but if it happen that his mother be also roaming about loose, both animals will go to destruction. And thus is it in the matter of the monk. If the body remain continually in its cell, the mind thereof will certainly come back to it after all its wanderings, for many reasons which will come upon it, but if the body as well as the soul wander outside the cell, both will become a prey and a thing of joy to the enemy."

Hermit in his desert cell near the Monastery of St. Catherine, Sinai.

When Abbâ Arsenius was in the palace, he prayed to God, and said, "O Lord, direct me how to live"; and a voice came to him, saying, "Arsenius, flee from men, and thou shalt live."

And when Arsenius was living the ascetic life in the monastery, he prayed to God the same prayer, and again he heard a voice saying unto him, "Arsenius, flee, keep silence, and lead a life of silent contemplation, for these are the fundamental causes which prevent a man from committing sin."

Hermitage in the desert near the Monastery of St. Catherine, Sinai.

Monasticism in Egypt

Otto F. A. Meinardus

The Coptic Orthodox Church is the independent church of Egypt. Most of the monasteries dealt with in this chapter and pictured in the photographs are Coptic monasteries; one, the monastery of St. Catherine in Sinai, is Greek Orthodox. Mark the Evangelist is regarded as the founder of Christianity in Egypt, in the first century. The new religion's early struggles were against the ancient practices of paganism and the influence of Hellenism and Greek philosophy, but it is events rather than theology that really set off the era of Egyptian Christians. The Coptic calendar begins with the year of Diocletian's accession to the imperial throne in 284, the beginning of the great suffering of the Coptic Church. No other early church within the Roman Empire was exposed to such violent persecution as the Christians of the Nile Valley. The dungeons were filled with some 500,000 men and women of all classes and stations in life, awaiting their turn for the rack and the gallows.

Religious toleration was finally established in the empire in 312, under the emperor Constantine. Egypt became an increasingly Christian country, with monasticism playing an important role in the development of Christianity as a social force in the country. In 451, following the Council of Chalcedon, which condemned the monophysite theology accepted by most Egyptian Christians, the church in Egypt broke away from the Orthodox Church of Byzantium and became fully independent.

Monasticism has been a part of Coptic Christianity since the early days of the church, and is enjoying something of a renaissance in modern times.

The Cradle of Monasticism

World Christian monasticism has its beginnings in Egypt. Attempts have been made to find the origins of Egyptian monasticism in several pre-Christian ascetic communities in Egypt, but whether these directly inspired the early Christian hermits must remain in question. There is no doubt, however, that one major reason for the withdrawal of the Christians into the desert was their periodic persecution.

From its modest beginnings on the edges of the desert the monastic movement developed into a way of life for tens of thousands of men and women. Within a few years of the founding of the new movement, Egypt became justly famed throughout the ancient world for the number of monasteries and the saintly lives of its hermits and monks. Strictly speaking, St. Paul the Theban, who died about 341, must be considered the first Christian hermit; however, the real originator of the monastic life was St. Anthony the Great, who was his junior by some twenty years. Born in 251, he settled in a mountain cave in the Wadi al-Araba in the Eastern Desert, some 60 kilometers from the shores of the Red Sea. Disciples settled in an oasis at the foot of the mountain, and the nucleus of the first Christian monastery was established by the middle of the fourth century.

Centers of monasticism grew up in three areas: the Eastern Desert; the Western Desert, especially Wadi al-Natrun; and Upper Egypt. In the forbidding wilderness of Wadi al-Natrun St. Macarius the Great established the Antonian form of monasticism, and in Upper Egypt St. Pachomius shaped it into forms that were later adopted by western counterparts. The Pachomian system subjugated the needs of the individual to the requirements of the community, governing the life of each monk by a precise set of rules and a code of discipline.

The Red Sea Monasteries

The monasteries of St. Anthony the Great and St. Paul the Theban were probably built about the same time, toward the second half of the fourth century. The original settlements consisted merely of the most essential buildings and many monks would have lived in solitary cells within walking distance of the communal worship center. But the early history of these monasteries is sketchy. A clear picture of their development emerges only in the twelfth and thirteenth centuries, with St. Paul's always existing to some degree or other in the shadow of St. Anthony's.

The Monastery of St. Anthony

By the beginning of the thirteenth century, the monks of the Monastery of St. Anthony had acquired considerable influence, and often determined even the policies of the Coptic Church. Throughout the Middle Ages the monastery provided many metropolitans and bishops. Its growing ecclesiastical significance is documented by the fact that at the ecumenical council of Florence in 1439, the Coptic Church was represented by Qummus John, abbot of the Monastery of St. Anthony, who signed the Act of Union, a document that united at least for a few days the whole of Christendom.

During the last decade of the fifteenth century, both Red Sea monasteries suffered severely at the hands of Bedouins who had lived as servants and gardeners within the walls. The Bedouins killed all the monks and destroyed the libraries. Smoke stains can still be seen on the walls of the Church of St. Anthony, where the usurpers set up their kitchen, lighting their fires with the ancient scrolls.

The monastery was restored in the first half of the sixteenth century, and there were Ethiopian monks at St. Anthony's from about 1520 to 1650. Sixteenth-century Ethiopian icons can still be seen in the monastery.

In 1622 a committee of cardinals was appointed in Rome to reunite the "schismatic Copts" with the Holy See of St. Peter. The efforts of Capuchin missionaries in the seventeenth century were followed by those of the Jesuits in the eighteenth, but neither group had much success. The missionaries did however acquire a number of important Coptic and Arabic manuscripts for the libraries in Rome and Paris.

The leadership of the Monastery of St. Anthony is especially noticeable during the seventeenth, eighteenth, and nineteenth centuries. Twelve Antonian monks became popes, and for almost three hundred years they determined the history of the church.

By the beginning of the twentieth century the monastery had forty-one monks. In 1928 there were almost a hundred monks, most of whom lived in the monastic dependency in Bush, north of Beni Suef. With the construction of asphalt roads to the monastery from the Nile Valley and from the Red Sea coast, a visit to the monastery became a popular family excursion, and today, cars and buses bring several hundred visitors at weekends. To meet these new demands, two new guest houses have been built.

The Monastery of St. Paul the Theban

The Monastery of St. Paul has always existed in the shadow of St. Anthony's. It is more isolated than St. Anthony's and has never attracted the same ecclesiastical and popular attention, partly because St. Paul never played a dynamic inspirational role in the Coptic tradition.

The medieval pilgrims of the fourteenth and fifteenth centuries unanimously state that the Monastery of St. Paul was dependent upon the monks of St. Anthony's Monastery. Like the Monastery of St. Anthony, St. Paul's suffered at the hands of the Bedouins who worked there as servants. Restorations were made, but a second devastation seems to have occurred in the latter part of the seventeenth century. In 1701 orders were given for the monastery to be rebuilt. The monastery received the same Capuchin and Jesuit missionaries as the Monastery of St. Anthony, as well as bibliophiles in search of ancient manuscripts.

In the eighteenth century the number of monks at St. Paul's varied between fourteen and twenty-five. Today there are approximately forty-five monks. Pilgrims from Egypt and from overseas visit the monastery because of Abuna Fanous al-Buli, in whom they see a charismatic healer and prophet. One night in 1975, several monks and visitors reported seeing a bright light ascend from the old cave church of St. Paul, remaining over it for some twenty-five minutes.

The Monasteries of the Western Desert

There is no indication that Wadi al-Natrun, or the desert of Scetis as it was known in Roman times, was inhabited until St. Macarius discovered there the quietness he had failed to find elsewhere. This area eventually became the center of Coptic monasticism, to which the great saints of the Egyptian church withdrew: St. Macarius, St. Bishoi, St. John the Dwarf, St. John Kame, and many others. Of the four monasteries of Wadi Natrun, two—the monasteries of al-Baramus and St. Macarius—are discussed and pictured here, alongside the Monastery of St. Samuel near Fayyum.

In the middle of the sixth century, there were said to be 3,500 monks in Wadi al-Natrun. In the ninth century, a source suggests that the Monastery of St. Macarius alone contained one thousand monks. Some of the figures are probably exaggerated—one reads, for example, that in the seventh century, some 70,000 monks saluted the Islamic general Amr ibn al-As. In any case, by 1088 only 712 monks lived in the seven monasteries of the Western Desert.

This whole period is marked by internal and external difficulties. At the same time as doctrinal disputes weakened the community internally, the monks faced a greater, external danger from marauding Berber tribes. The first destruction occurred at the beginning of the fifth century, but similar devastations took place through to the eleventh century, when Pope Shenuda II had protecting walls built around the monasteries.

The Middle Ages saw a rapid decline of the number of monks, which was no doubt further affected by the ravages of the Black Death. In 1710, in the four monasteries of Wadi al-Natrun, there were just twenty-three monks. In 1995, there were about   four hundred.

The Monastery of al-Baramus

The earliest settlement in the Desert of Scetis was in the vicinity of the present Monastery of the Romans, commonly called 'al-Baramus.' According to tradition, two sons of the Roman emperor Valentinian, Maximus and Domitius, the 'little strangers,' established themselves in a cell in the desert. It was said that the older brother achieved perfection before he died. Three days later the younger brother died. St. Macarius consecrated the cell and named it the Cell of the Romans. The earliest monastic community probably began around 340. Two additional patrons are especially commemorated in this monastery, St. Moses the Ethiopian and St. Isidore, whose relics repose in the principal church.

Like the other monasteries, al-Baramus suffered at the hands of Berber tribes, and was torn by theological disputes. In fact, throughout the Middle Ages two monasteries with the name 'al-Baramus' existed side-by-side, divided by Christological differences. By the seventeenth century only one survived. By the beginning of the eighteenth century, about fifteen monks inhabited the monastery, a number which by the middle of the nineteenth century had decreased to a mere four. During the pontificate of Cyril V (1874–1927), once abbot of the Monastery of al-Baramus, the number of monks increased to thirty. Major restorations were carried out, and the place became attractive to Coptic scholars.

In many ways the monks of the Monastery of al-Baramus reflect the new spirit that prevails in the Coptic Church. Combining prayer and study with farm and household chores, the monks also take on ambitious tasks such as land reclamation projects around the monastery. Constructional developments include the building of ten new cells, storerooms, a clinic, and a pharmacy, as well as a guesthouse and a center for spiritual retreats and conferences.

The Monastery of St. Macarius

The history of monastic life in the Desert of Scetis begins with St. Macarius the Great. Born around the year 300, as a youth he distributed his possessions among the poor and lived as a hermit. In a neighboring village lived a young girl who became pregnant. When she claimed that Macarius was the father, an angry mob came after him and almost beat him to death. The girl's parents intervened, however, saying he should be allowed to live in order to work and support the girl. Macarius humbly agreed to support the girl by making baskets and selling them in the marketplace. When the time came for her to give birth, she was in labor for many days, but unable to deliver the child. Finally, she confessed that she had slandered the monk, and identified the true father. It was only then that she was able to deliver the child. The entire village wanted to make amends to Macarius, but he fled into the desert to escape their praises.

Macarius's first cave was near the present Monastery of al-Baramus, where he offered guidance to the two 'little strangers,' Maximus and Domitius. After the death of the two princes he settled further south in the wadi, where a community of monks grew up around him. Macarius himself continued to live as a hermit until his death at the age of ninety.

During the middle of the sixth century, the Monastery of St. Macarius became the official residence of the Coptic popes and for several centuries remained the most important institution in the Desert of Scetis. It also became the pontifical necropolis, with no less than ten Coptic popes buried there. From the seventh to the thirteenth centuries, twenty-five monks of this monastery ascended the pontifical throne. In the eleventh century, the monks of St. Macarius's accounted for more than half of all monks in the Desert of Scetis.

By the end of the seventeenth century many of the monastery buildings had fallen into ruin, and a century later no more than four monks remained. The nineteenth century saw a slight improvement, but St. Macarius's remained the poorest of the four Wadi al-Natrun monasteries.

In 1969, a small group of monks was sent to settle in the Monastery of St. Macarius. Within two decades their numbers increased to over 120, most of whom were university graduates. New buildings now occupy an area six times that covered by the old monastery. Since 1975, the monks have reclaimed and cultivated large areas of the desert, and large numbers of people visit the monastery.

The Monastery of St. Samuel

This monastery is situated in the Qalamun desert south of the oasis of Fayyum. Its history can be traced back to the end of the third century. St. Samuel was not the founder of this particular institution, but rather the rebuilder of an old settlement. He lived in the seventh century during a period of severe persecution by the Persians and the Byzantines. Several times beaten and publicly flogged, he was eventually captured by the Berbers, but managed to escape. For fifty-seven years he lived as abbot of the monastery that was named after him. During his life the number of monks in the community reached 120.

The monastery flourished until the middle of the ninth century when it was devastated by the Arabs. It was rebuilt and by the twelfth century included twelve churches, abundant gardens, four large towers, and a high outlook. More than 130 monks lived there. By the fifteenth century, however, the situation had deteriorated. Historical information is scarce and it is difficult to know when the last monks abandoned the monastery; but it was probably some time in the sixteenth century.

The monastery was reoccupied toward the end of the nineteenth century when monks from the Wadi al-Natrun monasteries settled in its ruins. One of the great figures of the contemporary Coptic scene, the late Pope Cyril VI, served as abbot before he was elected to the pontifical throne in 1959. In recent decades the monastery has experienced a spiritual and architectural revival. The sanctuaries of the Holy Virgin, St. Misail, and St. Samuel have been renovated, and the walls adorned with neo-Coptic iconography. The monastery walls have been extended, and new cells and towers built.

The Monasteries of Upper Egypt

The Monastery of St. Shenuda or the White Monastery

The Monastery of St. Shenuda is situated on the edge of the desert four kilometers east of Sohag. The original settlement was founded in the fourth century by St. Pijol, the maternal uncle of St. Shenuda. St. Shenuda was born about 333 and is said to have lived to be 118 years old. He became the abbot of the monastery in 385. During the eleventh and twelfth centuries the monastery was inhabited by Armenian monks, and enjoyed a period of prosperity during which the church and the monastery buildings underwent several reconstructions. In the 1970s the monastery was reoccupied by Coptic monks, and was recognized by the Holy Synod as an 'official monastery' in 1997. It is popularly known as the White Monastery after the white limestone of its buildings.

The Monastery of St. Bishoi or the Red Monastery

The Monastery of St. Bishoi lies three kilometers north of the Monastery of St. Shenuda, in whose shadow it has existed since the fifth century. Though much smaller, the monastery was built on the same plan as the Monastery of St. Shenuda. The name Red Monastery comes from the color of the bricks used in its construction. The monastery was reoccupied by Coptic monks in 1980.

The Monastery of the Holy Virgin at Durunka

This new monastery was built in 1955 on a cliff shelf ten kilometers south of Asyut. The monastery is built into large caves that were once inhabited by Coptic monks and Christian refugees from persecution. According to a local Coptic tradition, the Holy Family visited the site on their flight to Egypt, resting in one of the caves. During the annual pilgrimage in August thousands of pilgrims assemble at the monastery. The residence of the bishop of Asyut is situated to the north of the sanctuary. Many new buildings for the accomodation of the pilgrims have been constructed on the hillside, and in recent years several visions of the Virgin Mary have been reported.

The Monastery of Saint Catherine

The Greek Orthodox Monastery of St. Catherine has a long and distinguished history. By the fourth century, the area around Mount Sinai had already become a focus for hermits seeking isolation and relative safety from persecution. In 337, St. Helena, the mother of Constantine, is said to have visited the hermits and to have ordered the construction of the Chapel of the Burning Bush on the site where God revealed himself to Moses. Two hundred years later, in 537, the Emperor Justinian built a fortified monastery and a church dedicated to the Virgin Mary, and soon after ordered the construction of the Church of the Transfiguration, "to the memory and rest of our late Empress Theodora." By the end of the sixth century, the monastery had gained international significance. By the middle of the ninth century Sinai had become an independent bishopric, and by the end of the eleventh was an archbishopric. In 1782, after disputes that started in 1575, the Monastery of St. Catherine became fully autonomous.

The tradition of the virgin-martyr St. Catherine only spread to Sinai in the tenth century, before which time the monastery was dedicated to the Transfiguration. Throughout the Middle Ages Ethiopians and Copts, Armenians and Georgians lived and died at Mount Sinai, and pilgrims from all over Europe made offerings to St. Catherine. The monks also received gifts from the kings and queens of Europe and the tsars of Russia.

Over the centuries, the monastery has had friendly relations with the Egyptian government, partly due to the need to ensure the safety of the Mecca pilgrims, whose route traditionally passed through the monks' territory. Men and women of all nations and ranks have visited the monastery, as one can see by paging through the visitors' book.

Text Sources

The texts accompanying the photographs, with one exception, are taken from *The Paradise or Garden of the Holy Fathers Being Histories of the Anchorites Recluses Monks Coenobites and Ascetic Fathers of the Deserts of Egypt Between A.D. CCL and A.D. CCCC Circiter Compiled by Athanasius Archbishop of Alexandria: Palladius Bishop of Helenopolis: Saint Jerome and Others*, translated from the Syriac by E. A. Wallis Budge and published by Chatto and Windus in 1907. The source of each extract is identified below by the book and section number (for example, I:3 is from Book I, section 3). The text on page 74 is from *The Desert a City* by Derwas J. Chitty, published by St. Vladimir's Seminary Press in 1966, and is reproduced by permission.